LAUNCH YOUR LIFE

Creating a Life in Service of God

ACTION PLANNER

Philip E. and Elizabeth J. Bruns

Carpenter's Son Publishing

Launch Your Life Action Planner

Published by Carpenter's Son Publishing, Franklin, Tennessee

Published in association with Larry Carpenter of Christian Book Services, LLC
www.christianbookservices.com

Cover Design by Carrie Bruns, www.carriebruns.com

Interior Design by Suzanne Lawing

Edited by Robert Irvin

Editorial Assistance by Michelle Diekmeyer

Printed in the United States of America

978-1-949572-76-6

To Elise, Carrie, Allison, and Rose:
you are more inspiring to us than you know.
PEACER!

Thank you for choosing to purchase the *Launch Your Life Action Planner.* We deeply believe that God has great plans for your life. We also deeply believe in the power of intentional living.

As you step back and consider where you have been, take stock of what you are currently doing, and make plans for your future, God will open doors for you and show you His purpose and plans for your life. The following journaling prompts, templates, and suggested work will help you dream, see how God has prepared you, and focus your energies. The book and *Action Planner* also offer practical suggestions to résumé writing, interviewing, and starting your career. This kind of work takes time and space. We also believe it can be helpful to share progress with a trusted friend, advisor, or mentor along the journey. Self-reflection, dreaming, and planning require putting it down on paper, meditating on it, and then picking it back up. We recommend actively working on it over some time.

You only have one life to live. Our desire for you is to live that life dreaming and living the purpose God has for you. Have fun.

Contents

I-P-A: WHAT IS THAT?

What one does is what counts, not what one had the intention of doing.

– Pablo Picasso[1]

Picasso was right. Without planning, intentions are just passing thoughts. Further, without the action, intentions and planning remain much-deliberated dreams. If you want to Launch Your Life, you need all three: Intention, Planning, and Action—or, *I-P-A*. If you are legal to drink and enjoy an occasional beer, you may be familiar with those three letters: I-P-A. But our I-P-A, *this I-P-A*—Intention, Planning, and Action—will provide you with many more life opportunities and benefits than an India Pale Ale.

While writing this book, we found several thoughts that touched our hearts in ways that challenged us in faith, action, and character. In the same way, we expect that you will find opportunities for growth in your character, spirituality, or life in general. Keep the thought of *I-P-A* at the forefront of your mind. Do you want to find a new college major or a new job? *I-P-A*. Would you like to enhance your career development or consider additional education? *I-P-A*. Have a desire to learn more about God's Word? *I-P-A*. Do you want to grow closer to God or a friend? *I-P-A*. Have other goals? *I-P-A*.

The *Launch Your Life Action Planner* will help you directly with the I and the P, and we hope it will inspire you on the A, but the follow-through is ultimately up to you. Heed Picasso's words as you read.

We want you to hear the call to faithfully move forward in life and feel empowered to do so. Imprint *I-P-A* on your heart, engrain it in your mind, and make it part of your soul. And where one door shuts, keep moving forward and look for another that opens.

If "plan A" in your action plan doesn't go as hoped, remember there are twenty-five more letters in the alphabet—and more than three thousand characters if you're in China! This book is not about your future. It is *for* your future. So let's make it count.

JOURNAL

✍ What is your intention with this Action Planner? Why did you purchase this book?

PART I

It Starts with God

Chapter One

DARE TO SOAR

Do you not know? Have you not heard? The Lord is the everlasting God, the Creator of the ends of the earth. He will not grow tired or weary, and his understanding no one can fathom. He gives strength to the weary and increases the power of the weak. Even youths grow tired and weary, and young men stumble and fall; but those who hope in the Lord will renew their strength. They will soar on wings like eagles; they will run and not grow weary, they will walk and not be faint (Isaiah 40:28-31).

This Isaiah passage is a favorite of many faithful men and women today. It's a Scripture that speaks of God's eternal presence and His unwavering power, and it carries a grace-filled promise for us. These are inspirational words about dreaming in Him. They also call us to go to God, lean on Him, and allow Him to change us into people who impact the world. We have hope as we pursue God, and specifically, hope to dream. In fact, because of Christ, we should be less afraid to dream. We should expect Him to use us and we should desire for Him to do things with our lives that only He can do.

It's easy to read about the dreams of others, to simply find a good story or an interesting read. We can sing songs about dreaming or listen to Dr. King speak his majestic words in the famous "I Have a

Dream" speech. But it's an entirely different matter to make things personal and go beyond being a dream spectator to participating in your own intentional work of realizing a dream.

God wants us to make things personal. He believes in us and wants us to dream. There is no more enduring inspiration than a dream that comes from God. The passage in Isaiah 40 is about dreaming. "Those who hope in the Lord will renew their strength"; "they will soar on wings like eagles"; "they will run and not grow weary, they will walk and not be faint." These are all inspirational words about dreaming. They inspire us to strive to make possible what we think is impossible. The challenge is to open our eyes to things not seen. They are God's words that give us hope of an extraordinary future and endless possibilities. But victorious dreaming takes passionate effort on our part. We need focused ambition and the ability to make deliberate decisions to realize a great dream.

As you launch into the early part of adulthood or the next stage of your life, think about your future. Where can God take you and what impact can you make that can only come from you? Where will you be in one year? Five years? Because there are so many variables in life, it is difficult to think about time much further than five years into the future. So for this work, we advise you to focus on dreaming in the one-to-five year horizon. The important thing is to realize that it begins with you. No one else can dream for you. For sure, you may have a loving parent, a close sibling, a friend, or a spouse who has high hopes for your future. And yet even if the whole world has high expectations for your life, your future comes down to you and your thoughts and choices for your life.

JOURNAL

Make a list of dreams for the next 1-5 years. What are your dreams:

Professionally?

Spiritually?

Scholastically?

Relationally?

The Wright Brothers were dreamers who lived by intention. Other visionary people had the same dream: to fly a controlled machine that could carry a man or woman. Four hundred years ahead of the Wrights, Leonardo Da Vinci created machine designs in hopes of flying, but he never saw success. In the years leading up to the notable day of the first successful flight in Kitty Hawk—December 17, 1903—there were others who made attempts to fly. In most cases, however, their efforts came crashing to the ground—often literally, sometimes ending their lives.

What was the difference? Why did the Wright siblings attain success where many others failed? Was their dreaming that much better? There are several reasons why fortune fell their way, but mostly it can be credited to their study of birds, their tenacity, and their application of bird flight to their flying machine. Despite the Wright brothers not being a story of faith that we read in God's Word, there are numerous principles we can take to heart. We know it took much study and preparation, as well as perseverance, to overcome the unknowns and failures. Before their time in Kitty Hawk, the brothers spent months reading and studying about birds. They would sketch and make numerous diagrams. This study informed experiments and prototypes to figure it out.

Beyond that, it took a bold non-traditional vision for them to move forward. There were no books to study on flying machines or airplanes, no information on the mechanics of wings or the effects of air pressure on an aircraft. The brothers were envisioning what no one else could. The Kitty Hawk locals enjoyed those same birds for many years, but only for entertainment. The Wrights saw a vision. They observed the birds with a desire to learn and create something that would leave an impact on this world. They dared to act on that dream. This vision led to deliberate efforts in each of their roles to make plans, communicate, and work efficiently. The brothers were willing to face the dangers, difficulties, and rough days. They also determined to keep after their goals and dreams when failure struck. They worked long hours crafting each part for the plane, and when those failed, they made new ones. They continued to persevere—more and more toward that splendid day when they would make their first flight.

JOURNAL

- In what ways are you willing or demonstrating an ability to face the challenges, difficulties, and rough days?

- What are the setbacks that you find create the most trouble for you in being able to move forward, with action and intention, toward your dreams? Why are they so difficult?

Because the phrase "dreaming for God" can be a bit vague, especially with what seems like a long future ahead, it's important to discuss productive dreaming and how it should show up in day-to-day living. The truth is that dreaming should touch every area of your life, and dreams should drive your day-to-day spirit and what you choose to do. We want you to recognize the gifts you have received from God, including your talents, experiences, and spiritual gifts and give them entirely to Him for His use. This surrendering to God should inform your college choice, your employment, your relationships, and more.

If you love God, you should dream that He uses your life in a way that fits with His will. The creator of all that we see wants to use you! This fact is simply incredible when we see and believe this.

JOURNAL

- What blessings, desires, or gifts fuel your dreams? How can you use them?

- What talents, interests, or abilities do you have from God that can drive your dreams?

But creating a path forward isn't easy. Even while dreaming, you'll need to overcome the traps and pitfalls that can jump in your path along the way. Dreaming of what God can do through you can be hazardous as well! On the one hand, dreaming can be the very thing that catapults your thoughts and efforts to impact the world for the better. But putting your heart and soul on the line, working hard, and spending hours working toward a vision—well, this also provides a chance to fail. And defeat can be discouraging, maybe even catastrophic. A failed dream can cause a large stumble, and without the heartfelt desire to get back up again, the soul can be left crushed and a goal can die. Perseverance and grit are ingredients for a lifestyle of dreaming. Humility, openness to our Father's discipline, patience, and waiting on God are all required in the journey of dreaming for Him. You should never forget that the nature of dreaming is inherently more difficult because it has additional obstacles that make it hard to persevere. These come from the one who is against you. Of him, Jesus said,

> *"The thief comes only to steal and kill and destroy; I have come that they may have life, and have it to the full"* (John 10:10).

The enemy is there. He has a plan to make life harder for you. He is definitely messing with you and your goals. He is against you and he is lying to you. Jesus could not have put it more plainly: "steal and kill and destroy." These are strong words. The enemy loves to deflate us, to take the very air from underneath our soaring wings so we fail and come crashing down. If you want to dream for God, it is a requirement to recognize this massive opponent and see the ways the thief works against you so you can overcome.

JOURNAL

✍Who are people you can connect with to overcome and get help? These are people who are spiritual resources and see your whole life in service of God. Who are they and in what ways can you use them to overcome, cheer you on, and seek advice?

✍List people who are secular resources and either in or close to the professional direction you believe God has put on your heart. Who are they and in what ways can they advise you about your career and profession?

The enemy is trying to destroy us through our thoughts. God has given you an inherent desire to do great things in a way that only you can, to dream about what you can do with Him and for Him. In God, you long to bring your entire self to the table whether you are an introvert or an extrovert, a man or a woman, and regardless of race, job, socioeconomic background, or any other personality trait or circumstance that defines you. In your heart, there is a yearning to be used by God, to be trusted by Him, and to fulfill your role as a purposeful Christian. You have a craving in your soul to feel valued by God. This is true for everyone, whether you are in the ministry, an electrician, an engineer, or simply working as unpaid mother or father. You know that God loves you deeply and sees immense value in you, so much so that He gave His Son on your behalf as a sacrifice for your sins. Because of this, you desire to be driven by that dream connected to your heart. Belittling thoughts and distracting ideas, however, get in the way. The enemy continues to fight against your hopes; he wants to crush your dreams and destroy any thoughts of changing the world for the better. These thoughts can run laps in your mind: you're too young, you don't know anything, you're not as spiritual, you're "not enough," "your future is nothing special," "just do your job," "just go to class," "just go to church," "you won't have an impact anyway." These are all simply lies. Recognizing them as lies will go a long way to moving them out of the way so you can plan and act on your dream.

JOURNAL

- What are some topics you can study in God's Word that can sustain you as you work to persevere? What are specific Scriptures that keep you focused on Bible truth versus lies from Satan?

Maybe you have thoughts like these and are having difficulty identifying a dream because of them. Perhaps you are avoiding dreaming because of fear or a specific failure. Too often we just avoid dreaming. It's easier that way. We may have a lot of non-dreaming peers around us, and this helps justify a stagnant lifestyle. There is safety in numbers. If everyone rolls a certain way, you feel comfortable rolling with them. It's just easier. Maybe avoidance has been caused by fear or past hurts. Maybe you were not believed in by important people in your past. Trampled dreams are not inspiring and they are no fun, so perhaps you avoid going back to that space again. You think extremely unhealthy thoughts. You see snarky memes online and then in your mind: "Maybe the purpose of your life is to warn others." Your thoughts move in this direction, and such thoughts resonate with you far more than healthy dreaming.

Unaccomplished goals are deflating as well. You've had inspirational ideas in the past, set hopeful goals for the year, or had optimistic plans for a semester. But goals weren't met. In faith, you tried again, but again you missed your goals. You tried a third time but struck out, and you aren't going back. You're tired of failure! You put up spiritual walls around you and hide in your cocoon because that is where you think happiness lies and where you can safely avoid dreams.

JOURNAL

- What spiritual help can you get from Scripture to ground you and refocus you in times of challenge or failure so you can better move forward?

Perhaps you have not been thinking about your future at all, the direction your life is going, your interests, or what lies ahead. Maybe you are just unsure how to think about the future, so you ignore what is ahead. While you don't say it out loud, you still like being a kid, and the thought of taking hold of your future, having dreams and setting goals, is too daunting, so you don't move forward. Thinking about your future can be intimidating, especially if it is a new concept for you.

JOURNAL

- What are some fears that plague you?

- List five Scriptures about fear. How does God's work help us face fear in a spiritual way? How does God offer to help us when we are afraid?

To overcome the fight that the enemy brings against you, you must look to Jesus and keep your eyes fixed there. We remind you of Isaiah 40 at the beginning of this chapter, of putting your hope in the Lord. We grow weary in our fight and it seems that the enemy is relentless. But the explicit promise in God's Word is that He will sustain you if you hope in Him, fix your eyes on Him, and if He is the anchor to your soul. Launching into your future with God all starts here. There is no step-by-step method to dream for God without having a focus on God. Think of the Wrights: all the work toward their dream focused squarely on creating a flying machine.

You shouldn't fight this fight alone; to do so is tiresome. Surround yourself with fellow dreamers for support. Allow God to work through others around you as you battle back against the schemes of our enemy. It is so encouraging and uplifting to see others gain success, have victories, and celebrate together. Sometimes God hands this encouragement to you, but many times it takes you reaching out to be a friend, and this can be difficult. In the same way that watching the Olympics may inspire you to begin exercising, we can be encouraged to dream by seeing fellow dreamers. Knowing this, Jesus sent out seventy-two (Luke 10) to go before Him to nearby towns and villages; this was a daunting task He gave them! He sent them out in pairs to support each other and be each other's cheerleaders. In the same way, you need helpers. You need fellow dreamers at your side engaged in their Christianity. This is how to put your future on the right footing!

JOURNAL

✍ Who are some fellow dreamers you can partner with as you move forward? How can you inspire each other in your dreaming? Reading this book and workbook together could be the kick start you both need! It can keep you both focused on God's Word, seeking His plan, and encouraging each other through your challenges.

Chapter Two

PREPARED BY GOD

For you created my inmost being; you knit me together in my mother's womb. I praise you because I am fearfully and wonderfully made; your works are wonderful, I know that full well. My frame was not hidden from you when I was made in the secret place. When I was woven together in the depths of the earth, your eyes saw my unformed body. All the days ordained for me were written in your book before one of them came to be. How precious to me are your thoughts, O God! How vast is the sum of them! Were I to count them, they would outnumber the grains of sand. When I awake, I am still with you (Psalm 139:13-18).

Maybe it was David's own child, or possibly one belonging to a family member. It's possible that holding a newborn baby in his arms could have triggered these thoughts from Psalm 139. As an adult, David saw God at work in his life in tremendous ways. David also recognized that God's work started in him before he saw light outside his mother's womb. He understood the omnipresence of God, and in a moment of humility, he realized that God deeply loved him since the beginning. More than his thoughts about himself, though, he valued God's thoughts, and he was ever grateful for God's early work in his life. It doesn't take much effort to see David's thankful heart and praising soul. And this gives us perspective as we begin our look at how God has been at work in our lives from before our first breath as well.

God started early in preparing you for something great. When considering your dreams and deciding to go after your future, do not underestimate the great things God has done in you already!

The next activity is meant to help you look at the spectrum of both highs and lows in your life and generate insights from your past experiences. God has prepared you through your experiences, and this will help you assess how God has used them for your benefit. You will start with the highs and then turn to the lows.

In this exercise, establish a beginning time and date with a memory of a **High Point** or **Key Event** in your life that was noteworthy in terms of positive feelings. Take this memory and flush out details around what your **Dreams and Goals** were at the time, the **People and Their Role** who were involved and what they contributed to this high point, and next the **Places or Context** that contributed to it being a positive event. Finish this with **What You Learned** in terms of insights about yourself and thoughts around how God has prepared you with these positive events.

HIGH POINT OR KEY EVENT - #1

Date

Dreams & Goals

People & Their Role

Places or Context

What You Learned

HIGH POINT OR KEY EVENT - #2

Date

Dreams & Goals

People & Their Role

Places or Context

What You Learned

HIGH POINT OR KEY EVENT - #3

Date

Dreams & Goals

People & Their Role

Places or Context

What You Learned

HIGH POINT OR KEY EVENT - #4

✍ ***Date***

✍ ***Dreams & Goals***

✍ ***People & Their Role***

✍ ***Places or Context***

✍ ***What You Learned***

HIGH POINT OR KEY EVENT - #5

✍ ***Date***

✍ ***Dreams & Goals***

✍ ***People & Their Role***

✍ ***Places or Context***

✍ ***What You Learned***

JOURNAL

✍ Stepping back and considering all the High Points, what insights do you have about yourself and how God has prepared you? Do you have insights when considering the people across all your events? Do the places or context have a pattern? Does the knowledge you learned have a pattern to it?

Before getting into the lows, it is worth a mention that there are lows that can be soul crushing or extraordinarily difficult to process and determine how God is working and preparing you. These things can include addiction, abuse, severe illness, and death. This handbook is not a substitute for professional counseling or other programs that offer healing mechanisms for some of these very difficult circumstances. We realize that the next exercise may have levels of difficulty for some readers and, even if the exercise is challenging, let it illuminate some next steps that you might take in addition to this handbook to facilitate your journey in seeing how God is preparing you.

Repeat the same process with the **Low Points** or times of failure or disappointment. Start with the earliest date, work your way through multiple events, and finish each with some summary thoughts regarding **What You Learned**.

LOW POINT OR KEY EVENT - #1

Date

Dreams & Goals

People & Their Role

Places or Context

What You Learned

LOW POINT OR KEY EVENT - #2

✍ ***Date***

✍ ***Dreams & Goals***

✍ ***People & Their Role***

✍ ***Places or Context***

✍ ***What You Learned***

LOW POINT OR KEY EVENT - #3

Date

Dreams & Goals

People & Their Role

Places or Context

What You Learned

LOW POINT OR KEY EVENT - #4

✍ ***Date***

✍ ***Dreams & Goals***

✍ ***People & Their Role***

✍ ***Places or Context***

✍ ***What You Learned***

LOW POINT OR KEY EVENT - #5

Date

Dreams & Goals

People & Their Role

Places or Context

What You Learned

JOURNAL

✍What insights do you have about yourself and how God has prepared you when considering the Low Points of your life so far? Do you have insights when considering the people across all your events? Do the places or context have a pattern? Does the knowledge learned have a pattern to it?

✍Are there low points that make you feel stuck in terms of seeing how God has prepared you, or do you see those low points as opportunities for growth and compassion toward yourself and others? What other steps, including counseling or programs, might you consider to help move you forward? We know this may be a sensitive subject for some. Please know that our purpose of this book and workbook is to walk with you on this journey and enable you to see dreams past your challenges. We want to inspire you to grasp your true value as God sees you while you continue learning from your past.

JOURNAL - Considering both the Highs and Lows together

✍What does this tell you about your personal strengths and weaknesses?

✍What kind of patterns or habits have you established that are helpful or harmful in terms of moving forward with a dream for the next stage of your life?

✍How has God prepared you for the next thing you are meant to do?

✍What does it tell you about the direction you'd like to go so that you can lean into your strengths, your interests, and where God has prepared you?

What David saw in the Israelite camp was a sad and hopeless situation in which the army, including some of his brothers, was just plain afraid. Grown men feared what they saw and chose to stand still. Unified in their fear, the status quo of the group was to do nothing, or, if anything, to run. If anyone had a renegade thought of meeting Goliath, no doubt simple logic applied by the others would have dissuaded him. *Who am I? I can't do it. I'm going to stick with the norm. I don't want to rock the boat.*

If one man asked another to join him, they talked each other out of it. Their spirits were disheartened, their faith had badly waned, and the downward spiral had taken over. Abstaining from any action at all caused their faith to dip even lower. Whatever training the Israelites had and whatever their fighting experience was, there was no one who felt confident to face this enemy. They did not see themselves as prepared for this battle. They all knew it and acted accordingly. At its core, the army was content to stay fearful and satisfied with complacency. Today, it may seem somewhat difficult to believe that no one could muster the courage to make the situation different—until the young David came along.

We have similar struggles, falling in with the status quo and settling for less. The spirit of complacency and satisfaction can cause long delays, even stop our dreams. When we are not engaged and not determined to focus on what is ahead, we can find ourselves in a swirl of self-inflicted defeat. We starve ourselves of inspiration. Fighting against complacency is a daily battle. Each day brings new challenges, and each day is another chance for the enemy to keep you in a downward swirl and drive you to forget about your dream to soar. Additionally, when an army of the complacent, those settling for less without any intention to follow through on dreams, surrounds us, it becomes even more difficult to rise up and be a dreamer. This world urgently needs more men and women like David. Do not be swayed by the non-dreamers around you. Stand up, keep working on your plane! God has prepared you to fly!

JOURNAL

- ✍Do you find yourself being complacent in areas of your life, generally? What about spiritually?

- ✍What are the forces around you that keep you from pushing forward, and what can you do to conquer and push past these forces?

At the head of this fearful army, Saul was the commander of the Israelites, and he led the way in apprehension. When Goliath made his taunts, Saul stood with his men, unable to muster the confidence in God needed to fight the giant. He knew about the experienced Goliath and he knew he was big. Saul faced a slew of opponents in the time since he became ruler over Israel. By the power of God, he punished the Ammonites, as well as defeated Moab and Edom, and routed other kings as well! With God as Saul's source of strength, he previously triumphed over the Philistines, a bitter enemy whenever there were ongoing battles. Saul had fought bravely and valiantly against many enemies in the past. But now, well, this was a different Saul. This Saul struggled, and he did not have the fearless confidence God had once given him. His prior success led him to his choice of disobedience to God (1 Samuel 15), a decision he would never overcome. Further, he simply doubted. He doubted his army would be victorious over Goliath and the Philistines. He doubted God. He doubted David.

Doubt is a real stumbling block. It clouds dreams and leads us to open waters with no destination in sight. With no direction, we find ourselves in a storm of doubt from which it seems impossible to move forward. It comes from two places: others around us and our own minds. There is a heavy influence of persuasion when a neighbor or friend doubts our abilities. We feel it, and it can come when we least expect it. It can come through something like a small comment or a noticeable eye roll. The doubters do not give us confidence. They provide us with uncertainty. They fill us with hesitation and insecurity. Their words or actions toward us take what we dreamed and believed possible and make it impossible. The world lives here. It's a dark and pessimistic place. There is little positivity. This environment fuels doubt in yourself and doubt in God as well. We struggle with hesitation, pulling back in our minds, telling ourselves what we can't do and what we can't accomplish. It's a battle, but you can fight against this negativity.

JOURNAL

- What doubts do you have that get in the way of dreaming your dream for God, and how can you replace these doubts with God's Word and God's promises? What specific Scriptures can you reference for help?

✍ Are you being disobedient to God and what you know to be the right thing according to His Word? What can you change? What Scripture can you use to help you be obedient to God's plan?

To the Philistines' credit, they sought to end this standoff. Twice a day they would attempt to end the battle as Goliath, a proud warrior, bravely stepped to the front to meet an opponent. He taunted and called them names; no doubt he had a booming, gruff voice. The Philistine hero looked terrifying. The description of him we read is quite extraordinary.

> *He had a bronze helmet on his head and wore a coat of scale armor of bronze weighing five thousand shekels [about 125 pounds], on his legs he wore bronze greaves [plate armor for the leg], and a bronze javelin was slung on his back. His spear shaft was like a weaver's rod, and its iron point weighed six hundred shekels [about 15 pounds]. His shield bearer went ahead of him* (1 Samuel 17:5-7).

No wonder the Israelite army was so unsure. It's probably fair to say that just the armor and weaponry he carried was enough for the Israelites to step back in fear. He was covered with armor from head to toe and backed by the entire Philistine army. It made the mountain of victory seem too tall to climb! The Israelites could not see a single part of the man that was vulnerable. Additionally, Goliath had a colleague, presumably shorter but also very strong, in front of him for the sole purpose of carrying his shield! The whole scene created a powerful vision in which no Israelite thought victory possible. Any hope of an attack was drowned out by what they saw and heard.

Isn't that just like our enemy, creating a dark vision of being dominated that thwarts any hope we have of gaining victory in our battles?

JOURNAL

- What do you view today as impossible? What are those things that make it seem like your dream is just not worth dreaming or that you are just not able to realize it? If there are tragic, extraordinarily difficult circumstances that are a part of your personal history, what can you do (counseling or other resources) to help you recover and once again be able to visualize your dream?

David had at least seven older brothers, some of which were tall and impressive, especially Eliab. Eliab was noteworthy enough that the great prophet Samuel, on first seeing him, thought he was the one to be anointed king of the Israelites and eventually replace the fading Saul. After God rejected Eliab, David's father brought in the rest of the older brothers for Samuel to consider as king. Once again, though, at God's direction, Samuel did not choose any of them. It was finally David—an initial afterthought—who was appointed as the future king. There were undoubtedly sibling battles before this time, and David's anointing probably served to drive a deeper wedge between him and at least some of his brothers. This wedge showed itself even more deeply when David came to the Israelite army asking about Goliath and the Philistines.

> *When Eliab, David's oldest brother, heard him speaking with the men, he burned in anger at him and asked, "Why have you come down here? And with whom did you leave those few sheep in the desert? I know how conceited you are and how wicked your heart is; you came down only to watch the battle"* (1 Samuel 17:28).

They had the same father, the same bloodline, and of all the relationships David had at this battlefront, surely his family would have been among his best and most supportive! But Eliab was angry, and he let David have a public lashing. He disrespected David and made false accusations about him in front of the men. Eliab questioned David's heart and his purpose. Behind it, there was unquestionably a heart of jealousy and bitterness. In our battles to dream for God, to strive to be used by God in any way He sees fit, sometimes it's the people closest to us who are the least supportive, or those who simply hurt us the most. Perhaps his own brother's comments were the most hurtful.

JOURNAL

- How have relationships been headwind for you in your dreaming for God? How can you be merciful, graceful, and yet move forward toward your dreams even when it may seem impossible? What Scriptures can support you in this?

Chapter Three

THE FOUNDATION FORMULA

He has shown you, O Man, what is good. And what does the Lord require of you? To act justly and to love mercy and to walk humbly with your God (Micah 6:8).

Buildings need firm foundations to stand. In earlier days, builders used cut stones or rocks to create the most stability they could, but the nineteenth-century invention of Portland cement enabled sturdier, longer-lasting footholds that we see in construction today. Foundations, either literal or figurative, are critical to sustaining anything long term. Jesus told a simple parable about this with the house built on the rock versus the house built on sand (Matthew 7:24-27). In that case, the foundation Jesus referenced was the context of putting God's work into practice in our lives. It stands to reason, then, that your relationship with God, your walking with God, is the primary thing that will help in the challenges, chaos, uncertainty, and emotions that will come as you launch your life and your dreams for God.

PRAYER

At the start of Luke 11, we see Jesus in prayer. Upon finishing, His disciples came to Him and asked Him to teach them to pray. Have you ever wondered why they did that? After all, is that a question you have ever thought of asking someone? Is prayer something more than the folding of hands, the closing of the eyes, and simply talking to God? The disciples may have seen their religious leaders pray, but there was something *different* in Jesus, something they had never seen before. The disciples regularly saw Jesus in prayer, and it became apparent to them how important it was to their Master. Jesus drew His strength and security from praying, and He let that time with God set His course. This was plainly visible to His disciples. In verses 2-4 of this chapter, Jesus teaches His followers details of prayer, including topics they ought to bring to God. In verses 5-13, however, Luke spends much more time recording Jesus' teaching on how God *answers* our prayers. Perhaps the disciples had spent time in prayer before, but it just didn't seem like God was answering their requests, or maybe it felt like God wasn't there. Perhaps they weren't experiencing the results to meet their expectations. It is interesting to consider that the disciples' inquiry about how to pray comes after watching Jesus pray! They weren't asking these questions while Jesus was talking to them about prayer. He was in the act of praying; He was setting the standard once again as He often did! In this example from Jesus, we see His prayer life providing a higher call to His disciples, and they wanted to figure out how He did it. They wanted the details because there was something they saw making a difference for Jesus. In a teaching opportunity sometime after the Luke 11 account, Jesus instructs His disciples more deeply on prayer.

> *Then Jesus told his disciples a parable to show them that they should always pray and not give up. He said: "In a certain town there was a judge who neither feared God nor cared about men. And there was a widow in that town who kept coming to him with the plea, 'Grant me justice against my adversary.' For some time he refused. But finally he said to himself, 'Even though I don't fear God or care about men, yet because this widow keeps bothering me, I will see that she gets justice, so that she won't eventually wear me out with her coming!'" And the Lord said, "Listen to what*

the unjust judge says. And will not God bring about justice for his chosen ones, who cry out to him day and night? Will he keep putting them off? I tell you, he will see that they get justice, and quickly. However, when the Son of Man comes, will he find faith on the earth?" (Luke 18:1-8)

Luke puts it plainly in verse one. Jesus told this parable because He knew His disciples would be tempted to give up during prayer. It applies to us as well, and Jesus knew this. We need this parable to remind us to keep praying and not give up. Deep, meaningful, and persistent prayer challenges our faith. We know His word teaches us that He is attentive, but we don't always see the answers to our prayers, especially in the timing we think is appropriate (or needed). We see in Jesus' illustration, also known as the Parable of the Persistent Widow, that the widow is continually coming back to the judge and crying out for justice. Jesus is quick to note her passion, her persistence, and her mind-set of refusing to give up in a situation far from ideal. It took extra effort. Jesus teaches how God longs to bless His chosen ones through prayer.

JOURNAL

- What are the specific prayers you are praying about your life, your dreams, and your future?

✍Do they include prayers for being used by God in your future, and in what way?

✍What prayers has God already answered for you in steps you've taken that have brought you this far?

✍What types of things hinder your prayers? How are you creating habits to overcome those obstacles?

BIBLE STUDY

Everyone has a favorite Bible character, but these people are much more than mere individuals, and the Bible is more than a mere book. Sometimes, if we remember the people in the Bible were folks just like us, it helps the words jump off the page and come alive. These were people who lived, walked, and breathed. The men and women we read about in Scripture made mistakes, got angry, and had to go to sleep each night just as we do. They got grumpy on their bad days and shouted for joy when their lives were blessed. Have you ever imagined what the twelve disciples discussed with their wives and families the evening after they watched a herd of pigs run off a cliff? What did it look like when the shepherds saw the angels singing in the night sky? How would you have responded? Imagine what it must have been like to load the donkeys and begin walking with Abraham not knowing where he was going. Would you leave everything if you were in his situation? Envision the faith and transformation in Peter as he stood before thousands to tell the story of how their sins crucified Jesus. Was he scared? Would you have been afraid? Picture the humbling, bright-light moment when Saul talked with Jesus by himself—and soon after became Paul. Are you willing to make a crazy change like that?

The people in the Bible are inspirational, motivating, and they lived as examples to move our faith today. Their stories are there to impact our days, give substance to our lives, and spur us to greater heights in our faith. Their written accounts come to life so we can believe in Jesus, that He is the son of God and the Messiah. The descriptions are there for us to internalize, visualize, and imitate, not to gloss over. We don't need to know the type of fruit Adam and Eve picked, only that they each took a bite. What kind of large fish swallowed Jonah doesn't really matter, just the fact that he survived to teach about God, at God's direction, in the wicked city of Nineveh. Jesus' life should inspire us and build our confidence that, through Him, we have all we need.

I seek you with all my heart; do not let me stray from your commands. I have hidden your word in my heart that I might not sin against you. Praise be to you, O Lord; teach me your decrees. With my lips I recount all the laws that come from your mouth. I rejoice in following your statutes as one rejoices in great riches. I meditate on your precepts and consider your ways. I delight in your decrees; I will not neglect your word (Psalm 119:10-16).

These verses were written by an author who was passionately devoted to God's Word, and that passion is evident throughout all of Psalm 119. The importance, the eagerness, and the profound longing are there, clear for the reader to see. It begs a question: is this your heart? Do you have excitement for God's Word that rivals a young child's Christmas enthusiasm opening his or her gifts? Is there eagerness in your heart to dwell on His ways? Do you think about His words at night? What do your actions tell you?

God intends for us to engage in His Word as the treasure that it is, but time can do odd things to all of us. As we age and become increasingly more familiar with the biblical stories, we can arrive at a place where we are distracted, uninspired, and our time with God lags. Reading the familiar story of David defeating Goliath can turn into only mildly encouraging words instead of deep inspiration from God that stirs the heart.

God knows us. He knows our weaknesses. In His mercy He offers His Word to us. God's gift is meant to be pondered, trusted, leaned upon, and remembered. His words are intended to direct us, give us answers, and bring us peace. Consider:

My soul is consumed with longing for your laws at all times (Psalm 119:20)

Your statues are my delight; they are my counselors (Psalm 119:24).

Direct me in the path of your commands, for there I will find delight (Psalm 119:35).

I will speak of your statutes before kings and will not be put to shame, for I delight in your commands because I love them (Psalm 119:46, 47).

I have considered my ways and have turned my steps to your statutes (Psalm 119:59).

Your word, O Lord, is eternal; it stands firm in the heavens (Psalm 119:89).

Your word is a lamp to my feet and a light for my path (Psalm 119:105).

Because I love your commands more than gold, more than pure gold, and because I consider all your precepts right, I hate every wrong path. Your statues are wonderful, therefore I obey them (Psalm 119:127-129).

Great peace have they who love your law, and nothing can make them stumble (Psalm 119:165).

It's crucial to see the ongoing need for God's living and active Word in your life, to see the impact it can have, and to keep it as an anchor in your daily living. There are countless great books about God and spiritual principals, but none of them can—nor should—replace God's Word and our time in Bible study.

JOURNAL

- What topics in your Bible study are inspiring you about your future?

- List three Scriptures and how they have changed your life.

- List some Bible verses you believe can help you to move forward. Consider your career, your character growth, as well as what may be holding you back in terms of taking a hold of your future.

- What are you learning about your character as you study the Bible, and how does this inform your plans going forward? What Scripture can you reference to grow in your character?

- If you are struggling in your Bible study, journal some about that. Is it hard to find time? Is it a discipline you long to develop? How can you stay inspired?

PERSONAL MINISTRY

> *"Neither do people light a lamp and put it under a bowl. Instead they put it on its stand, and it gives light to everyone in the house"* (Matthew 5:15).

> *"Now that the Lord your God has given your brothers rest as he promised, return to your homes in the land that Moses the servant of the Lord gave you on the other side of the Jordan. But be very careful to keep the commandment and the law that Moses the servant of the Lord gave you: to love the Lord your God, to walk in all his ways, to obey his commands, to hold fast to him and to serve him with all your heart and all your soul"* (Joshua 22:4, 5).

God intends for us to be a bright light. That light comes from our love and devotion to the Lord our God. Consider the Israelites after they crossed the Jordan River to the land promised them by God. Joshua probably knew the temptation that would come upon them, so he reminded the people to be careful, to love, to obey, and to walk with and serve God with all their hearts.

This reminder holds just as true for us today. If you're a Christian, you probably go to church regularly and may attend other services and activities through the week as well. Church activities exist for us to be encouraged, to see friends, to sing songs, and to worship, but they are not enough to fulfill the call to be a light on a stand. We live in a lost world that has endless needs. God calls us to a lifestyle that echoes the life of Jesus—and Jesus spent much of His life ministering to sinners, the sick, and the poor. His time with His "church," or disciples, was often spent in the environment of sinners, the sick, and the needy. And just like Jesus, we must have the lost and the needy on our hearts, spurring us to specific actions and a specific lifestyle. We need to have a personal ministry, a ministry in which we are actively reaching out to and giving to others.

Having a personal ministry is much, much more than offering an invite for a Sunday service. It is being the lamp on the lampstand and living in a way that your neighbors and friends see you as a beacon of light. It is about having integrity in the workplace or keeping a godly attitude when someone else gets credit for your work. It is about having respectable character, about being the one who has a genuine concern for the coworker who has a sick mother or asking the classmate about their vacation. It is about being a hard worker, or an excellent employee, or a top-notch business owner, or being an honest example for others. It is about having God as your ultimate priority, about having your home or apartment an inviting haven so you can offer an invitation for dinner or maybe host a double date. It is also about an invitation to come and worship with you or to come to your home for a Bible study. Jesus saw the masses of people as helpless sheep. He saw the spiritual needs as well as the physical needs, and He offered Himself. Having a personal ministry is about love, encouragement, and offering hope. And when the time is right and God opens the door, you will be the help for the person who needs God, just like the criminal who turned to Jesus.

JOURNAL

- Define three aspects of personal ministry in your own words. How do you think these will affect your dreams and future if you put them into practice daily?

✍ What parts of your personal ministry feel easy? Which ones are harder for you? Why?

✍ How can you serve your classmates or coworkers?

✍ How can you connect with the poor in your area?

✍ How can you directly impact five people close to you who are not churchgoers?

✍ How can you meet needs in your community (remember Mark 12:41-44)? Here are some ideas: Collect nonperishable food items from neighbors for a food drive/toy drive, organize a group to volunteer at a food pantry or other benevolent organization, organize a group to clean up trash and invite people to church, organize a group to give blood, have a block party (or apartment complex party) so you can meet all your neighbors and build friendships with them.

✍ How can you better meet the spiritual, physical, or emotional needs at your church? Consider who you can encourage in spiritual growth or faith, someone you can meet a physical need with by delivering a card, sandwich, or other service, or who you can encourage that may be struggling with illness or grief.

PART II

You and Your Intention

Chapter Four

THE COMPLEX YOU

The first three chapters of this book are about your dreams, your past, and your connection with God as you formulate an intentional direction for the next phase of your life. This chapter is about the present, complicated you. You will examine how you spend your time, do a self-assessment of your strengths and opportunity areas, and narrow down dreams into concrete thoughts so that you can start working toward a specific plan. Your solid foundation is built on God, your personal ministry is in place—and now we move forward to integrating your dream with God's dream.

Your reading and journaling thus far have primed you for this evaluation of your current life. You are grounded in dreams and knowing how God has prepared you. You also have a sense of how the enemy slows you down or has inhibited your dreaming. We believe intentional living comes from a deep connection with God and letting God lead you while you are grounded in the Word, assessing yourself in the present, and making concrete steps toward specific goals for the future.

You are a complicated person and you have a complex life. Additionally, God has a plan for the next chapters of your life. As you take stock of the complex person you are, we advise you to focus on what is calling you and the positive aspects of your talents and abilities. While keeping in mind any spiritual headwinds, weaknesses and challenges, we only use them for informational purposes—not to beat ourselves up. Armed with your dreams, talents, and knowledge of strengths and weaknesses, it is easier to make forward progress toward your dreams. We believe wholeheartedly that you will fill out a full, God-centered life as you spend more energy on the positive aspects of your life versus the things that produce headwinds.

With that as context, let's look at how you are spending your time and examine how well it suits you, what gives you energy, what motivates you, and if there are things about how you are spending your time that you would like to change.

You can start by looking at the big blocks of time that you have during a week. In a typical week, you have about 100 waking hours. Each of the sections of the pie chart below represents five hours. Start with blocking your typical week into sections like Work, Church, Family, Free time, etc. After creating the bigger blocks, color them and label them (an example pie chart follows).

Weekly Time Spent
5 Hours Per Slice

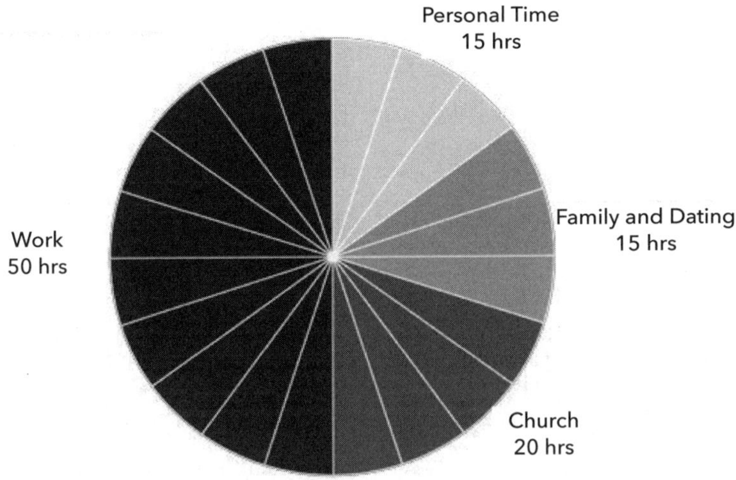

JOURNAL

What kinds of things give you energy when you consider how you are spending your time in a typical week?

✍ What kinds of things fuel your sense of balance and purpose?

✍ What motivates you and drives you when you feel a job or activity is well done?

✍ Thinking again about the categories for how you spend your time in a typical week, rank order them from highest satisfaction to lowest satisfaction and journal a bit about why you rank them in the order you have chosen.

Satisfaction	Category	Hours per Week	Insights About High Versus Low Satisfaction
High			
Low			

JOURNAL

- ✍ What would you like to change when you look at your satisfaction and insights?

There are forces at play in your life that can propel you forward or hold you back. It's good to have a sense of those forces and the ones that are driven by you as well as the ones that are driven by your environment. This next exercise is a self-assessment about these forces. Start with the ones that are about you or the internal forces. They are your individual **Strengths** and **Weaknesses**. Next, move on to the environmental or external forces. Those are the **Opportunities** as they present themselves to you and **Threats** that could limit the future path you see in your environment.

SELF-ASSESSMENT

INTERNAL–IT'S ABOUT YOU

✍ Strengths: what are your current strengths?

✍ Weaknesses: what are your current weaknesses?

EXTERNAL–IT'S ABOUT WHAT IS AROUND YOU

✍ Opportunities: what positive opportunities are in front of you?

✍ Threats: what challenges do you see coming your way?

Now that you have completed a high-level assessment of the complex you, positives as well as opportunities, please use the following journaling prompts to start formulating concrete goals you can explore for your future. These prompts are meant to move beyond dreaming and into concrete goals that you can pursue with a resume, job search, and networking.

JOURNAL

- Think about the careers and jobs that are well suited to the insights you have gathered so far. Do these careers and jobs not only match the qualifications you may have, do they also match your talents, what gives you energy, and your gifts? Please note if you need more training or experience to pursue this career or job and declare next steps in your specific goal-setting in Chapter 8.

✍ Who do you know in the same general career space that you desire, and what kinds of questions could you ask them about moving into that career field?

✍ How can you begin to network with people in that field beyond individuals you already know? Identify things like professional events, job fairs, electronic career possibilities, networking sites (i.e., LinkedIn).

Chapter Five

YOUR BRAND EQUITY

Whatever you do, work at it with all your heart, as working for the Lord, not for men, since you know that you will receive an inheritance from the Lord as a reward. It is the Lord Christ you are serving (Colossians 3:23, 24).

Brands are everywhere. They each represent something; they call to us. If you stop and stand at a busy downtown street corner where there are cars and stores all around, you'll find yourself surrounded by branding. Each car and truck has a unique look and has branding on the front, back, and sides. You'll find that you covet some of those vehicles. Others? Not so much. You would also see a variety of stores, their signs in plain view. They may have big sale signs on the windows and brightly colored flags waving in the wind trying to grab your attention. Brands vie for your attention and even cause a reaction on your part. For instance, which would you choose: Pepsi or Coke? Do you prefer Twitter, Snapchat, Facebook, or Instagram? Is it Starbucks or convenience store coffee when you are on the go? For clothing, would you choose H&M or Forever 21?

Believe it or not, like stores and products, people are brands too. For any person, their character is their brand. For example, did you have a "class clown" type in your high school? Is there someone at your work who is known as "the quiet one," or is there a "party animal" in your friend set? What people say and how they say it, how they act and carry themselves—all of this drives their brand.

Have you ever thought about being a brand? What do you think the people around you would say about you, your character, or your brand? Think of it regarding brands you already know, both positive and negative. Let's say you are a Nike, General Electric, Sony, Apple. What makes those brands work, or not? What do you expect from your favorite brands, and why are they your favorite brands? Now turn your attention to you. How do people experience you? Can people count on you to bring your best in whatever you do? What brand attributes describe you: honesty? integrity? being on time? hardworking? service-oriented? Or, with any of those things, are they not the case? Through God's Spirit, you have a chance to be a brand that people want to hire, reward, and develop. You have a chance to create the ______________________________ Brand in ways that can move you forward in life. You can be a brand that people will come to appreciate and desire as well.

JOURNAL

✍ Think about the value you want to bring to your profession or future employer. Great branding is about delivering a benefit that is of great value. You have ways you can contribute in terms of your education, your character, and your innate skill set. Journal about the benefits you want to bring professionally. If you are struggling with this question, list your strengths and how those may translate into benefits for your employer.

- Job searching is complicated and competitive. Think about the ways you contribute to your current employer or a future employer that are totally unique to you, the things that make you special, the things that make you stand out in a crowd when lots of other people are going for that same job. If this is not clear, ask someone close to you how they think you are unique or may be specialized for a certain trade or profession.

✍Think about specialty areas of your life—individualized ways you approach something or something you do which makes you feel proud of yourself. What do others know you for, or what things strike your areas of passion? Focusing on your strengths and passions is a great way to approach your branding.

✍Think about your current situation, either in school or in a job. What would your coworkers say about you? Consider both the positive and the negative. Consider skills, talents, and character qualities.

✍ Now, consider the branding thoughts you've journaled so far. Do the branding thoughts about who *you want to be* match with your *current situation*? If they are not the same, what steps can you take to move toward the ideal branding you want?

✍ Create a sentence or two (no more than fifteen words) about what you want your branding to be. Make it powerful. Make it uniquely about you. Consider how it will make you stand out from the crowd. This idea should inspire you about how you interview and how you carry yourself in your profession because it will allow you to create a narrative about yourself in the workplace.

✍ Consider the verse below (from Colossians) and journal how you are doing in these areas: "whatever you do," "all of your heart," and "as working for the Lord." How does this help you in terms of the direction you would like to take your brand?

Whatever you do, work at it with all your heart, as working for the Lord, not for men, since you know that you will receive an inheritance from the Lord as a reward. It is the Lord Christ you are serving (Colossians 3:23, 24).

✍ "Whatever you do" is about reliability and consistency of your brand. Great branding is always consistent. You want your whole life to be in service of God and to represent that no matter where you are or what you are doing. Does your whole life reflect the branding you want when considering your life as a disciple of Jesus? In what ways are you consistent? In what areas could you improve?

- "All your heart" pretty much speaks for itself. In what ways is it easy to give all your heart? In what ways or circumstances is it harder to give all your heart?

- "As working for the Lord." The gospel is good news and you are meant to share it. How can you use the circumstances of your life, combined with your branding, to drive your personal ministry? What ideas do you have in which you can use your gifts and abilities to meet needs? Or how can you use your life to reach out to people? How else can you use your whole life for God?

PART III

Taking Action to Move Forward

Chapter Six

PRACTICAL PLANNING AND SPIRITUAL CHOICES

"So I say to you: ***Ask*** *and it will be given to you;* ***seek*** *and you will find;* ***knock*** *and the door will be opened to you. For everyone who asks receives; the one who seeks finds; and to the one who knocks, the door will be opened"* (Luke 11:9, 10).

Everything starts with the Alpha and Omega. We began this chapter with memorable words Jesus spoke to His disciples as an answer to their question about how to pray. We highlighted certain words because of the importance of understanding the depth of Jesus' statement. The three words—**ask, seek, knock**—are action words. If you want the door opened, you raise your arm and knock on God's door. If you want to find, you open your Bible and seek God. If you want to receive, you open your mouth and ask God. God blesses people around the world daily, according to His will, without being asked. But Jesus speaks very clearly in these words that He hears our specific prayers as we pour out our hearts to God. We don't just pray to be blessed, however. We pray to connect with the creator of the universe, the one who gave us life and breath. We connect so we can better understand ourselves, our purpose, and the God we serve. It's likely you are reading this book to search God, know His heart, and grasp His meaning for your life. That begins with talking to God and asking, seeking, and knocking.

In your prayers, go after it! Start with a decision to have a humble heart and be open to God's answer. Ask God for clear direction in your life so you can make great choices. Pray that God will move in such a way that you can see the barriers that may hinder your progress and have the wisdom and strength to overcome. And decide to never, ever quit.

JOURNAL

- How much do you pray, and when do you pray about your future?

- What are you specifically asking of God to move forward in your life? Having a list of the direction you need, the doors you want to open, and the topics where you need wisdom are great things to regularly pray about as you are trying to move forward in your life. As you put your specific requests in front of God, your prayers will support you moving forward to the other points of seeking and knocking.

- Consider asking for hard things as well: to understand how you need to change, for God to reveal His purpose and plan for your life (even if this is not what you think it should be), to see how you can contribute to the world as your whole life is in service of Him.

- After asking for God's help, where are you knocking? What doors are in front of you where you are intentionally knocking? Knocking requires thought, intention, and action.

To complement the idea of asking, seeking, and knocking in your prayer life, God has put people in your life to help. We recommend a thoughtful approach to getting advice from qualified people around you. Think specifically about your decision space and who can help. Depending on your needs, some people are better suited for information than others. For instance, would you want to get advice on a college major change from someone who has never attended college? Would you seek financial help from someone who is irresponsible with money? Two easy examples, right? The answer to both questions is "of course not." Therefore, consider your source. Talk to people who are already in a successful career path you are considering. If you are changing majors or careers, find others who have made that move successfully. If you are having trouble overcoming an obstacle in creating your future, find a person who has overcome a similar barrier. If you need help in finances, find someone who manages money with excellence. We mention this because it can be easy to settle for the convenient friend for empathy, sympathy, and advice rather than the person who can help you move forward. Inevitably, talking to more than one person will yield different opinions and information. Receiving multiple views is an excellent strategy to help you consider the big picture (Proverbs 11:14, 15:22, 24:6). Consider your sources and their advice and do your best to make the best choices. You are the one who will live with the decision, and the great news is that God is always at work within those choices, teaching us and strengthening us along the way.

JOURNAL

- Make a list of advisors with whom you would like to connect in the coming months regarding decisions you are trying to make. Consider the topics of career, relationships, finances, and spiritual growth.

RELATIONSHIPS

All of us have a wide variety of memories from our childhood. Some had a lovingly supportive upbringing, others less so, and some faced significant trauma in their childhood. Whether you come from a single parent home, have stepparents, foster parents, guardians, or traditional mothers and fathers, there is one aspect of parenting and guardianship that has become an obstacle for many. We want to address it here.

As you grow and mature, those who helped you when you were younger may be having a difficult time letting go, or you may be having a hard time growing into an adult relationship with that authority figure. It is probably not a coincidence that the rise of "helicopter parents," or guardians of that same nature, hanging on longer than they should coincides with the growth of the information age. Parents and their children have instant access, all the time, to what each other are doing and experiencing as they grow. This access can cause difficulty when the child is growing into an adult and needs to make her or his own decisions, reap the consequences of those choices, and develop character and a life path. Parents may over-involve themselves in activities, responsibilities, and choices that adult children should be making more independently. This continued engagement can lead to the adult child second-guessing their decisions, being paralyzed by fear, and generally "waiting for life to show up" instead of moving forward with established intentions.

JOURNAL

✍ Are there aspects in your life planning in which you may need to step back and think differently about your future when you think about relationships? Are there relationships that you need to reevaluate or step back from that are holding you back?

- If so, how is this holding you back? What respectful approach can you take to move you forward? We know from Scripture we must honor our father and mother (Exodus 20:12; Matthew 15:4) and we also recognize healthy boundaries can be challenging. If you need help in your authority relationships and healthy boundaries, consider asking older mentors how to approach this subject.

Having a mentor or older advisor is very much a biblical concept. Timothy confided in Paul as a mentor, and the twelve disciples looked to Jesus, of course. Your trusted relationships should include one or more people you look to for advice, and not just friends. If you are still taking classes at your university, the school will often provide academic and employment advisors for you. Some companies also help facilitate a mentor, and you will do well to take advantage of such opportunities. Your church may facilitate a relationship or two for you. It helps, however, if you take it upon yourself to first see your need for mentoring and then pursue relationships in that capacity.

Let's consider this Oprah Winfrey statement:

"Mentors are important, and I don't think anybody makes it in the world without some form of mentorship." —Oprah Winfrey[2]

First, understand your need and the advantages of a mentor relationship. With Oprah so successful and living as an inspiration to millions, why would she want or need mentors? The truth is that wisdom from experience is irreplaceable in career, life, and character development. And what an advantage! It is not like you are the first one to live, have troubles, or face the need to make big decisions. Everyone lives through difficult experiences, and many are willing to pass on what they have learned.

If you find yourself in a job without a mentor, ask your boss who he or she might recommend. Even if you are not in your career job, seek to establish relationships with people who are in your desired field. These are networking opportunities that can build bridges to future employment, provide excellent references, and more. Building relationships like this will enhance your employability as you learn about your field and the needed ingredients for success. Additionally, having others in your church advise you as you grow spiritually is a must. Look to those in your ministry who you admire as well as those ahead of you in life who you respect. Remember to ask, seek, and knock! Chase after those relationships and set up regular times with those valuable people in your life. Then allow God to work through those you trust.

- Make a list of potential mentors. Initiate a request to see if they would be willing to serve in this capacity. When making the request, tell the potential mentor what you would like to gain in this relationship. Be specific about your expectations and be flexible as you move forward with them. (For instance, you may expect them to be able to get together twice a month, but they are only able to meet once per month. Accept that with grace.) Consider the gains of the relationship and work with them as you build the friendship.

In the twentysomething culture today, it seems the casual "taking a girl or guy out on a date or double date" is a bit under attack. Perhaps it is a combination of TV shows and movies, as we mentioned earlier, or the enormous ease, availability, and debilitating use of pornography that are among the worst contributors to this mind-set. Or perhaps the decrease in actual face-to-face social interaction of growing adolescents and young adults is a culprit as well. So often men and women feel they are in the "friend zone" and take it personally when they do not instantly match with an interest. Sometimes we think we should live in an online environment where someone falls in love with us at first sight. Some apps allow men and women to utilize impure pictures to acquire or keep an interest. These worldly influences and dynamics produce lies of expectations and extreme discouragement when desires are not met. They also encourage impurity and immorality to build intimacy. Simply put, these enemy tactics do not work and are against God's laws and will. We recommend plenty of casual and double dating to build a genuine friendship that God can grow into a romantic one.

✍ What strategies are you specifically using to maintain purity and a godly focus in your dating life?

✍ What are your expectations around dating and do these expectations fit with godly perspective? Spend some time reflecting what the world, media, and social media tell you about dating, romance, and marriage. Research what the Bible says on these topics. Where are there mismatches, and what can you do in your life to live according to the Bible?

RÉSUMÉ, INTERVIEWING, AND JOB SEARCHING

As mentioned before, we believe you can land a job that is in service of God's plan for your life on the premise of ask, seek, and knock. These thoughts in Luke suggest proactive, intentional work on our part to allow God to open a door, and they are applicable to set your course in your life and career.

Let's talk résumé first. We believe there are two primary requirements for writing a great résumé. First, you must know who you are (in the big context of your life) and how God has prepared you. Second, you need to do the work it takes to represent that *you*, brilliantly, in a one-page document. You must represent yourself so well that your résumé is noteworthy and attractive. Often it will need to stand out relative to hundreds of other résumés.

Sometimes we want the magic light bulb to come on and illuminate the perfect job, or we think it's a simple ask and then our desire just shows up from God. In the end, you must do the work. Think about James 2:17: "In the same way, faith by itself, if it is not accompanied by action, is dead." And James 2:22: "You see that his [Abraham's] faith and his actions were working together and his faith was made complete by what he did." Asking requires us to know ourselves and know what to ask of God. You need to be grounded in the details of your ideal job so you can pray specifically. Seeking requires extraordinary effort to go after something and persevere when achieving it isn't easy. You may face rejection in job searching, disappointment in not getting an interview, or you may advance as far as being the second choice when there is only one job available. Regardless, remember this: knocking implies putting yourself out there and taking a risk. You need to cast a wide net of applications to land a job that contributes to a growing résumé.

There are many resources available for résumé writing. This book wasn't written with the goal of being an authority on the subject. Instead, our book attempts to help you capture the whole version of yourself, including those Christian and discipleship character qualities that are the traits needed to make you both attractive and desirable as a hire. Our goal is not to help you evangelize or proselytize through your résumé. Instead, our goal is to help you create a résumé that represents your gifts and spiritual qualities so the reader gets a sense of your character. Your character has positive attributes that are spiritual and include an upward call to righteousness. Those attributes are desirable to potential hiring managers.

Many times, when we (Phil and Beth) look at the first drafts of résumés, we see a list of generic tasks that describe a basic job. Many times, those jobs may not be the kinds of experiences that jump off the page for hiring managers. We also find that successful résumés usually speak to two things: first, why a candidate is valuable because of his or her character; second, why the listed jobs suit the candidate's strengths.

Having a résumé that speaks to godly qualities like patience, perseverance, generosity, great work ethic or attitude, service, appreciating people, and so on, are great to highlight. It makes your résumé a story about the ______________________ Brand rather than just a list of tasks you did in generic jobs or service experiences. As you add character to your résumé, you will cut through the clutter of the resume stack to get called in for an interview because more of you is on the page. Be confident that your godly character matters in a job over the long haul. It makes you more interesting in a résumé and will separate you from that stack on the hiring manager's desk. You have gifts, talents, and character. Your job is to make them come alive in your résumé.

In terms of some basic guidelines:

- Keep your résumé to no more than one page.
- Have a good balance between white space and words. Too much white space and you aren't that interesting. Too many words, your résumé is hard to read and a turn-off as soon as someone looks at it.
- Represent yourself as well-rounded with job experiences and internships that are in your field, service work, and leadership

experiences. If you haven't had any experiences to date that are close to or in your field, we recommend looking for an internship or volunteer experience now. That way, you can add that to your résumé in the next version.

- Consider a résumé section on skills that capture unique people skills, coursework, or technical skills to make you stand out or illustrate that you are qualified for the position you are seeking.
- Some section headers that work include: Work Experience, Service Experience, Education, Coursework, Skills, Awards, Recognition, Activities. If it isn't obvious looking at your résumé what kind of job you are looking for, consider adding an Objective statement at the top of your résumé.

EXAMPLE RÉSUMÉ #1

Nicely Engineered

University Address:
2355 Chickens St.
Ann Arbor, MI 65897

nicely@xxxxxxx.com / +1 (012) 345-6789
nicely.weebly.com
www.linkedin.com/in/nicely-eng

Permanent Address:
3502 Hanna Ln.
Murphy, OH 81550

EDUCATION

University of Michigan, Ann Arbor, MI — Graduation April 2015
Bachelor of Science, Chemical Engineering — GPA 3.72
Minor in Spanish
University Honors Program, Dean's List

WORK EXPERIENCE

***Process Engineering Co-op,* Johnson Pharmaceutical, Detroit, MI** — Spring-Summer 2014

- Became one of three primary process engineers on a $250 million dollar project covering: PIDs, PFDs, fluid flow modeling, material balance, scope activity definition
- Gained valuable experiences in a wide range of engineering disciplines such as: HVAC design, structural design, equipment specs, project delivery, project scheduling/budget, electrical design
- Trained key client's process community in aspects of plant design (PIDs, PFDs, and layout drawings) with three other trainees. Offered to adjustments to the coursework for future classes.

***Product Design Co-op, App. Engineering Co-op,* Ed's Super Technologies, Buffalo, NY** — Fall 2014, Summer 2013

- Initiated development of water treatment designs for beverage applications. These designs bridged the gap between sanitary and industrial systems and served as a baseline for future development.
- Worked with experts in the field to compile mechanical and electrical component lists, size pumps, and analyze different parts of reverse osmosis, activated carbon systems, and multimedia filters. Designs were technically impacted at an international level to assist in global standardization.
- Completed budget and firm proposals for clients. Contacted suppliers within and outside of the company to assemble proposals and job cost information. Assisted in over $700,000 in sales.

***Product Development Co-op,* Millie Company, Grand Rapids, MI** — Spring 2012

- Developed test methods, placed consumer tests, analyzed and interpreted data for feminine hygiene products. Made initial strides for the project in setting requirements for the project to move forward.
- Worked with flexibility/agility to reframe problems, navigate systems, and embrace changes, broadening the study from just using the product in-use to the application/initial perceptions of the product.

ACTIVITIES

***Volunteer,* World Helpers, United Kingdom; Philadelphia, PA; India; Fiji** — 06/10, 06/11, 12/11, 12/12

- Selected for a global leadership team for multiple 2-week service trips
- Completed service activities in the community such as cleaning up schools, running children's programs, raising money for orphanages, painting a local hospital, counseling at a camp for inter-city girls.

***Member,* National Youth Council, World Helpers, Miami, FL** — 7/11 - 5/13

- Planned service events multiple times a year and coordinated volunteers for the Cincinnati area.

AWARDS

Greatest Scholarship — 2010

SKILLS

- Excellent at organizing, leading, taking initiative, flexibility/agility, prioritizing, working within deadlines, accuracy
- Public speaking skills, four years of Spanish
  Proficient in Microsoft Office and AutoCAD, basic knowledge of MATLAB, RStudio, and AFT Fathom

EXAMPLE RÉSUMÉ #2

Ima Goodone
2588 Corell Cr
Arcadia, KS 63512
012-345-6789
imagoodone@xxxxx.com

Summary

Experienced leadership in relational and corporate environments achieving goals through developed and executed plans, resulting in personal and business growth

---

Experience

Student-Intern, St Peter Church – Arcadia, KS 2015-Present

- Trained to encourage and mentor others in the church with heavy emphasis on group leadership, planning, and organization
- Collaborated with leaders to discern best care practices for members
- Lead through experience, inspiration, and personal example to help others through challenges and team building
- Planned and lead group events for 50-70 people including social activities, teaching, and food planning
- Public speaking to crowds of 400 with ongoing opportunities
- Traveled to 4 other universities with similar responsibilities

Manager, Jack's Subs – Arcadia, KS 2014-2016

- Lead business to nearly 400% of increased sales
- Coordinated with other allied businesses to create additional sales opportunities
- Organized and procured suppliers to ensure sufficient food supply per event
- Created new procedures that increased efficiency and directly led to other business opportunities
- Problem-solver in customer, technical, weather adversities, and often working extra hours
- Trained multiple employees in business processes regarding health and food regulations
- Sole manager of the business owner's absence

Shipper - Plainer, KS 2012-2013

- Successfully completed jobs with co-workers in shipping industry
- Acquired skills to efficiently complete tasks under time restrictions
- Adapted to working both first or second shift when needed

Key Skills

Communication, ability to work under pressure, self-motivation, leadership, teamwork, adaptability, resourceful, purposeful, helpful, and supportive

---

Education

Bachelor of Science in Science May 2017
University of Northeast Kansas, Arcadia, KS

Creative use of action words enhances a résumé. As you fill in details of your experiences, start the bullet points with interesting, empowering action words. Don't use boring words like "did," "was," or "completed." Instead, use higher impact verbs and descriptive words like "achieved," "improved," or "managed." If you can monetize your contribution in some way with a number, incorporate that in the bullet point. For example: "Improved the customer base by 20 percent by exceptional customer service and relational skills"; or, "Initiated and created a sales system so that the volume of widgets sold increased by 40 percent." Each experience you list on your résumé should tell a small story about the ______________________ Brand to cause the reader to want to interview you about it.

Here is a chart about monetizing the contribution and good-versus-bad verbs when explaining your experiences.

- Value the contribution somehow
  - Increase
  - Decrease
  - Expanded in What Way
- Use numbers
  - Percents
  - Dollars
  - Growth - Clients, Customers
  - Other Results

Good	Bad
Achieved	Did
Improved	Was
Trained/mentored	Utilized
Managed	Participated
Created	Completed
Resolved	Responsible for
Volunteered	Value-add
Influenced	Experience working in ...
Negotiated	Worked
Launched	Assisted

As you draft your résumé, reach out to your mentors. It can be quite helpful if they have previously hired and fired employees or if they are in or at least close to your field. Beyond résumé input, ask these people if they know of open jobs or places to search for jobs in your desired field. As you do that, these relationships can grow into networking and mentoring relationships that can fuel your career going forward. Remember to reach out to people who will tell you the truth and offer constructive feedback. Take the extra step that others don't when looking for a job. Let mentors review your résumé and help you practice interviewing. Embracing the people who will give you honest and open feedback will set you apart and give you an advantage.

As you finalize your résumé, start planning and practice interviewing. Good interviewing involves preparation on two fronts. First, be prepared to answer questions and tell the story about why you are the right person for the job. The hiring managers want to know what you can do to make their company better. Second, be knowledgeable about both the job and the company where you are applying. Demonstrate this knowledge in the interview by offering questions. Good hires are a win-win for both parties. Good interviews have a balance of dialogue about you as well as about the job. This balanced dialogue leads to both parties being able to see if you are a strong match for the position. If you show up at an interview only prepared to discuss yourself, the interviewer will feel the discussion is one-sided and that you think the job is all about you. Even worse, you could portray yourself as if you think they are doing themselves a favor by hiring you. That pride will be evident and get you nowhere. When you demonstrate knowledge and curiosity about the job, company, or organization, the interviewers will know you have done your homework and that you have given thought to how you are going to make a difference if they hire you.

As mentioned, you should prepare well for interviews including finding a coach, mentor, or supporter who can practice a mock interview with you. Practicing your answers multiple times, out loud, with another person will help your confidence, succinctness, and coherency. Here is a preparation list to consider for interviewing.

- Prepare answers to questions you may be asked. Here's a basic list:
  - o Tell me about your greatest achievement.
  - o Tell me about an obstacle, how you overcame it, and your approach.

- o Why did you apply for this job?
- o What are the three of the most important things that you would bring to this job?
- o How would your current boss describe your work and contributions?
- o What and how would your skills contribute to this company?

✍ Research the company, making a list of the attributes you find attractive, ways you think you can contribute, and questions that demonstrate your knowledge of them. This will help you decide if you want that specific job and shows the potential employer your knowledge and interest in the company.

✍ Do an assessment of why the company should hire you. What specifically can you offer in the interview to highlight this thought?

✍ Prepare to describe two strengths and one weakness. Choose strengths that represent the core of who you are. You may have discovered these in this workbook so far and how they are a good match for the job with which you are interviewing. Choose your weakness carefully. You don't want your weakness to be a fundamental requirement for this job (or else this job may not be a good match). If you share the weakness in the context of how you are growing, that can be a good way to deliver it in an interview.

✍ Prepare a list of questions that you can ask. For example:

- o What does the company or organization value the most? How would my work fit with the company's goals?
- o Can you give me examples of the most and least desirable aspects of your company culture?
- o How does the company value and measure success?

- o What kind of processes are in place for me to work collaboratively? To receive ongoing training?
- o What is the most important thing I can accomplish for the company in the first sixty days of my employment?
- o What do you enjoy most about working here?

- Dress appropriately. If you don't know the appropriate dress code, ask someone.
- Take a few copies of your résumé.
- Be early.

Lastly, you need to consider how to find out about and access potential jobs. Job searching is difficult and it takes a lot of work. Here are some thoughts:

- Consider career fairs both at school as well as in the community. When going to a career fair, dress appropriately and take copies of your résumé. Treat every person you meet as if they are a potential interview, where you can offer your interest and your experiences as you explore a job fit for you. Research the companies at the career fair prior to going so you can introduce yourself in a knowledgeable way.
- Establish a professional presence on LinkedIn or other job search websites. Search and network on a regular basis to find connections and jobs.
- Network with others you meet who are close to or in your field. Ask them if they know of job openings. Offer your résumé to them and ask them for feedback. Ask them to consider keeping an eye open to find potential jobs for you.
- Attend networking functions (professional organizations in your field).

FINANCES

We have discussed how your whole life is in service of God, not just the religious part. Your view of your finances and how you handle them is part of that equation as well. Your view of money is about your character and how solid you are on your foundation. There is nothing wrong with money, having it, or even having plenty of it. But the choices you make as you launch your life and continue to grow older will expose where you genuinely store your treasure. Your character will drive your decisions on things like giving back, making purchases, and saving for the future. Will you be both wise and generous with what God has given you?

In your day-to-day finances keep a simple budget. It does not need to be much, just a simple tool that tracks what you spend. Get a folder and begin saving your receipts for the month. Keep every receipt, from fast food to phone bill, from loans and cable bill to gifts and traveling. Make sure you have any credit card statements and bank account statements handy as well. Everything that has to do with finances should be in that folder from the first day of the month to the last.

Next, we suggest a simple spreadsheet with the weeks listed on the vertical column on the left side and your spending categories across the top. With each category list your target budget amount for expenses for the week. Leave the box beside it blank, then fill it in with what you spent. The spending categories should include gas, food, utilities, rent, clothing, phone, insurance, car payment, contribution for your church, and savings. For example, if you want to keep forty dollars per month for a trip you are planning next year, be sure to put that in your budget. Important: your spending should always be less than the money you have or are planning to spend.

Here's an example:

	Clothes	Food	Auto Gas	Fun	Rent	Church Contribution
Aug 1						
Aug 8						
Aug 15						
Aug 22						
...						
...						
...						

Chapter Seven

JOURNEY ON

By day the Lord went ahead of them in a pillar of cloud to guide them on their way and by night in a pillar of fire to give them light, so that they could travel by day or night. Neither the pillar of cloud by day nor the pillar of fire by night left its place in front of the people (Exodus 13:21, 22).

Many are the plans in a man's heart, but it is the Lord's purpose that prevails (Proverbs 19:21).

Joseph's journey is truly applicable for both life and career. His life reflects the proverb above as we see God work—and we see God work through deep human disappointment and failure. You'll see God's hand come to life through both those who honor God and those who do not know God, all to fulfill a promise.

We discussed God's preparation in our lives and how, in His great wisdom, He lays the groundwork for our future. It is in that spirit that we begin our lesson of Joseph, starting about four thousand years ago in a very different time and culture. For Joseph, the story begins with a conniving grandmother and her son, and through the love story of his mother, Rachel, and his father, Jacob.

Joseph grew up in a cloud of dysfunction, including: the loss of his biological mother, stepsiblings who were jealous and hated him, stepmothers who also likely resented and possibly even hated him, and just a general culture of deceit and manipulation that ran deep within his family. If you have grown up with dysfunction like any of this, you know how difficult it is to see God's sovereignty when family life is so difficult. Joseph's life had many challenges from this point forward. His past, his family, and his circumstances provided him the opportunity to go to God, trust God, and surrender his strife-filled family to God. Ultimately, all this dysfunction was in service of God's plan for the Israelites, which is incredible. God uses all challenges for His glory if we follow Him and stay faithful like Jacob and Joseph. Let's use the next few pages to capture ten lessons from Joseph's life.

LESSON ONE: Persevere through your past, take what is good into your future.

Give thanks to the Lord, for he is good (Psalm 136:1).

JOURNAL

✍ Take some time to consider the situations where you have persevered. These circumstances contribute to character that God will use in your career and life journey. Write about how they will help you in the future. They may affect your goals, personal brand equity choices, or ways you can contribute at your workplace going forward.

LESSON TWO: "Pit" days will come.

How long, O Lord? Will you forget me forever? How long will you hide your face from me? How long must I wrestle with my thoughts and day after day have sorrow in my heart? (Psalm 13:1, 2).

JOURNAL

- Besides perseverance, what will you need to get through your "Pit Days" that will come?

- Make a list of Scriptures that can be your truth and your rock when the "Pit Days" come your way.

LESSON THREE: Let your life show your gratefulness to God, not just your lips.

> *I will exalt you, O Lord, for you lifted me out of the depths and did not let my enemies gloat over me. O Lord my God, I called to you for help and you healed me. O Lord, you brought me up from the grave; you spared me from going down into the pit. Sing to the Lord, you saints of his; praise his holy name* (Psalm 30:1-4).

JOURNAL

✍ How do people around you see your gratefulness?

✍ Make a list of ten things you are grateful for when considering your journey going forward.

LESSON FOUR: Always take the high road, the road of integrity.

I know that you are pleased with me, for my enemy does not triumph over me. In my integrity you uphold me and set me in your presence forever (Psalm 41:11, 12).

JOURNAL

- If you are being challenged with compromising your integrity or you are tempted to do so, spend some time journaling biblical perspective as well as how you can fight against this temptation. As with Joseph, having integrity when it is hard can really distinguish you in your professional development and Christian walk.

LESSON FIVE: Life isn't fair, but you can still shine.

In God, whose work I praise, in the Lord, whose work I praise, in God I trust; I will not be afraid. What can man do to me? (Psalm 56:10, 11).

JOURNAL

- How do you feel about this statement?

- What biblical strategies can you employ when you face injustice or unfairness? What Bible verses can support you?

LESSON SIX: Be willing to take part in hard conversations.

May integrity and uprightness protect me, because my hope is in you (Psalm 25:21).

JOURNAL

- What is the hardest part of hard conversations for you?

- If you have hard conversations coming in your near future, write a plan on how to approach and find a mentor to contact on this topic.

LESSON SEVEN: Take time for self-assessment.

Search me, O God, and know my heart; test me and know my anxious thoughts. See if there is any offensive way in me and lead me to the way everlasting (Psalm 139:23, 24).

JOURNAL

- How can knowing yourself in a better way help?

✍ Ask three friends to help you with self-assessment by getting input in the top three areas that can help propel your professional life forward. Journal what you learn.

LESSON EIGHT: Grow your résumé by building skill sets and experiences.

Create in me a pure heart, O God, and renew a steadfast spirit within me (Psalm 51:10).

JOURNAL

✍ Journal the specific skills, training, or experiences you can commit to learning or growing that are "résumé worthy" in the next six months.

LESSON NINE: If you keep your eyes open for opportunities, they will come.

"But now, Lord, what do I look for? My hope is in you" (Psalm 39:7).

JOURNAL

✍ Are your eyes open? What opportunities are you looking for in the next year?

LESSON TEN: You'll never go wrong with love and humility.

He guides the humble in what is right and teaches them his way. All the ways of the Lord are loving and faithful toward those who keep the demands of his covenant (Psalm 25:9, 10).

JOURNAL

✍ Would your classmates or coworkers use these words to describe you? How can you grow in them?

Chapter Eight

THE LION AND THE GAZELLE

Architecture starts when you carefully put two bricks together. There it begins. —Ludwig Mies van der Rohe[3]

The quote above is fitting to start the last chapter of the *Launch Your Life Action Planner* as there is always a first brick when erecting a building. Even the greatest museums, longest bridges, and tallest buildings started with the first brick. Another brick was put on the first brick, another after that, and another after that. Step by step, piece by piece, individual materials create a greater project. No structure on earth has been created otherwise. Stacking those first two bricks together is like the initial effort you take as you begin building your career at the dawn of your adult life. A life is built brick by brick, by trying and then regrouping, self-assessing and making a change, and always having forward progress.

JOURNAL

Establish three goals with specific next steps that you want to accomplish in the next three months to Launch Your Life forward.

Commit to praying about them every day and working to make them happen every week.

Goals to Move You Forward in the Next Three Months

✍ ***Goal 1***

✍ ***Next Steps***

✍ ***Goal 2***

✍ ***Next Steps***

Goal 3

Next Steps

What happens if you give up building midway or decide not to push through to completion for one reason or another? What happens if you get tired or frustrated and decide to stop engaging in bricklaying? Imagine the 1,250-foot Empire State Building having only been started, with bricks stacked only to your waist. While the initial effort is crucial for launch, your continuous determination will carry you forward and set you apart.

Although its origin is unclear, an African proverb inspires us to take this daily approach.

> *Every morning in Africa, a gazelle wakes up. It knows it must run faster than the fastest lion or it will be killed.*
>
> *Every morning in Africa, a lion wakes up. It knows it must outrun the slowest gazelle or it will starve to death.*
>
> *It doesn't matter whether you are a lion or a gazelle: when the sun comes up, you'd better be running.*

Even if you have never set foot in Africa, the picture is clear, the message is poignant. The lesson regarding your career, your faith, and your life is to keep moving forward each day. As you do, you will continue to grow.

JOURNAL

Following your three-month goals, establish goals with next steps that you want to accomplish in the next six months to Launch Your Life forward. What needs to be true for you to make these happen?

Six-Month Goals

✍ ***Goal 1***

✍ ***Next Steps***

✍ ***Goal 2***

Next Steps

Goal 3

Next Steps

You may have a list of things you would like to improve or change as a result of reading this book, and you may also be overwhelmed a bit. It's quite understandable! Reflect back to the Preface of this book and the acronym *I-P-A*. Intention, planning, and action. Incorporate *I-P-A* into your thoughts moving forward in one area. As you develop your dreams and goals, God will work with you. As you work on implementing your plans, God will work with you. Consider the stories of Peter, David, or any of the many biblical men or women discussed in this book. All continued to lay their individual bricks until something more significant was built. As each of them planned,

God helped them grow. When they dreamed, God helped them live. They were the lion. They were the gazelle. And their stories speak to increasing passion and grit as they built their full life and character in service of their God.

> *Within your temple, O God, we meditate on your unfailing love. Like your name, O God, your praise reaches to the ends of the earth; your right hand is filled with righteousness. Mount Zion rejoices, the villages of Judah are glad because of your judgments. Walk about Zion, go around her, count her towers, consider well her ramparts, view her citadels, that you may tell of them to the next generation. For this God is our God for ever and ever; he will be our guide even to the end* (Psalm 48:9-14).

The writer of Psalm 48 had his eyes and heart open; he knew his place in creation as well as in God's story. The author goes further than just praise in this psalm, however. The writer seems to be well along in years, as if speaking from personal experience. As we read above, it is more than a direction to sit and ponder God's glory, although that can be helpful. The writer uses the action verbs "walk," "go," "count," "consider," "view," and "tell" in ways that echo the heart and life of the impressive Proverbs 31 Woman. It is a call to exert physical energy toward seeing and understanding God. This expended energy will secure your beliefs and pay your faith forward in ways that will naturally inspire those who follow in your footsteps.

Don't dream, plan, and live without God. Others around you will do so, and some will seem to have great success. But don't be fooled. Besides letting God work through your life and career during your time on earth, both your goal and God's goal is for you to spend eternity with Him. Until then, the Psalm 48 writer gives us a great promise. After several direct words of praise, even calling God the Great King (v. 2), the writer rests his final comforting thoughts on the eternal existence of the creator and the unfailing engagement of God in our lives. Although written well after the time of Joseph, it seems the once-despised teenager could have written these very same words.

JOURNAL

Following your three- and six-month goals, establish goals with next steps that you want to accomplish in the next year to Launch Your Life forward. How do they fit with your skill set and past experiences, and with God's plan for your life?

One Year Goals

✍ ***Goal 1***

✍ ***Next Steps***

✍ ***Goal 2***

Next Steps

Goal 3

Next Steps

For us, the promise in Psalm 48 is the same. Ever present in our lives, God will escort those who walk forward on the path, His path. Each step forward represents experiences that can produce a new view of God. And while the short view may either encourage or discourage, keep your eyes on the long path ahead and *always find a way to move forward*. Toward the end of your long journey, you will have a magnificent story to tell.

Notes

1. Goalcast, "The 20 Pablo Picasso Quotes to Inspire the Artist in You."
2. Ong, "Famous People Who Have Benefited from Mentors."
3. Brainy Quotes, Ludwig Mies van der Rohe Quotes.

About the Authors

Philip and Elizabeth Bruns are Christians in the Cincinnati, Ohio area and have led several groups of singles and parents for more than thirty years. Phil and Beth are the founders of Launch Ministry (www.launchmini.com), have designed and facilitated multiple workshops, and travel the country speaking to young parents, parents of teenagers, and single professional groups.

Phil and Beth have several mentoring relationships established with both married and single professionals to coach résumé writing, including the self-assessment work required to have a great résumé and interview. They also help in job search, networking, and career navigation. They focus on times of transition, and their classes emphasize the full life, including faith, marriage, family, career, and academics, all in service of God. As an extension on the idea of transition, they also work with new parents and parents of teens to teach parenting with purpose. Their work helps with building child and teen character, faith, identity, and the family journey for the long haul. They use both biblical and modern-day stories as examples for inspiration.

Professionally, Phil has extensive domestic travel experience and has had successful careers in real estate and construction, holding contractor licenses in five states and serving multiple Fortune 500 clients. Beth has extensive foreign travel experience and has a successful career as an Engineering Research Fellow working in the area of research and development.

They have four faithful adult daughters who have launched or are launching their careers.

For More Information and Resources

You are invited to contact Launch Ministry
www.launchmini.com or email the authors
at hello@launchmini.com
You are also invited to follow Phil and Beth at Launch Mini
on Facebook, Instagram, and YouTube